Contents

Introduction

Hercules (HUR-kyoo-leez) was one of the best-loved and most famous heroes from Greco-Roman mythology. Hercules was made a servant to the evil king of Tiryns (TIER-inz) for twelve years. In order to win his freedom, Hercules had to perform some very difficult tasks for the king.

Here are two of the 12 labors, or tasks, Hercules did in order to secure his freedom.

Hercules and the Deer

Hercules did well on his first two tasks, which angered the king. The king gave Hercules a third task that was sure to make trouble for Hercules. He asked Hercules to bring the goddess Artemis' (AHR-tuh-mis-iz) pet red deer to him.

Artemis was the goddess of the hunt. She loved
all animals and was their protector. But this deer
was the most special of all to her, for its horns
were made of gold and its hooves were made of
bronze.

Hercules dreaded this job because he knew that
Artemis loved her deer, yet he had no choice but
to follow the king's orders. So Hercules set off on
foot to find Artemis' deer, which lived in a forest
fifty miles away from the kingdom of Tiryns.

After traveling many days, Hercules came to the
forest. He was tired, so he sat down by a river to
rest. And what should he see but Artemis' deer!

6

Hercules leapt to his feet. He pulled out his bow and arrows, but then he thought about how angry Artemis would be if he hurt her deer. He chased the deer instead, hoping to catch it without hurting it. Of course, deer can run much faster than people, and it got away.

Still Hercules did not give
up. He continued tracking
Artemis' deer, day and night,
for over a year. He chased
it through dark forests,
up steep mountains,
and across roaring rivers.

8

He chased it in the
sweltering heat of summer
and in the deepest cold
of winter. Each time it
seemed Hercules might be
able to grab the deer, it
gave a mighty leap and
disappeared.

At last, the deer got so weary of running that it stopped to rest by a mountain stream. Hercules had tried to catch the deer so many times, only to fail, that he decided to see if he could wound it and stop it in its tracks. He didn't want to harm the deer but had to think of some way to keep it from running away.

So Hercules drew out his bow once again.
He put in the arrow and pulled back the string.
Zing! The arrow sailed through the air and hit
Artemis' deer in the shoulder.

Hercules jumped from his hiding place and
raced to the deer. He picked it up and slung it
over his shoulders. Then he began the long
trek back to Tiryns.

12

But before Hercules got out of the forest,
Artemis found him. She was furious.

"What do you mean by hunting my deer?"
Artemis asked. "Don't you realize this is the
only one like it in the entire world?"

"Yes," answered Hercules humbly. "I've tried for
over a year to catch it without harming it,
but I couldn't do it."

Then Hercules explained to Artemis about the king of Tiryns. He told her about the jobs he was required to do, and how he couldn't be free until he completed them all.

Artemis took pity on Hercules. She took the deer from him and tended the wound until it healed. Then she gave the deer back to Hercules, who brought it alive to the king.

So it was that the third labor of Hercules ended.

Hercules and
the Augean Stables

The king of Tiryns assigned Hercules many more
difficult tasks, but the smelliest of them all was the
fifth one. The king ordered Hercules to clean out
the stables of King Augeas (aw-JEE-uhs) in just
one day. That wouldn't have been so bad except
that Augeas had thousands of cows, and he kept
them in stables that had not been cleaned for
over thirty years! But compared to the other jobs
Hercules had completed, this one didn't
seem so bad. Besides, Hercules had a plan.

Hercules went to Augeas and offered to clean out his stables in only one day. But there was a catch: in return for doing this, Hercules wanted Augeas to give him one-tenth of the cows. Augeas thought Hercules would fail to get it done in one day, so he agreed.

Augeas' son went along with Hercules to see how
he would accomplish this seemingly impossible
task. Hercules studied the stable yard wall and
then knocked a huge hole in one side of it. Then
he went to the other side and made another hole.

Augeas' son scratched his head in puzzlement.
What could Hercules be thinking? He was
soon to find out.

Once he'd finished making the holes,
Hercules started digging. He dug deep
ditches that led from two rivers
straight to the holes in the walls.
The rivers rushed down the
ditches, then into one hole
and out the other.

20

All of the filth was washed away.
The stables were clean for the first
time in over thirty years!

When Augeas tried to cheat Hercules out of his reward, Hercules took him to court. Augeas' own son told the judge he'd heard his father's promise to Hercules, so Augeas was ordered to give Hercules the cows he had been promised.

To celebrate the happy ending to his fifth labor, Hercules sponsored a series of games. Boys came from all around. They ran races and wrestled and drove chariots for days on end. Some people say these games were the very first Olympic Games.